Fall In Love with the Beloved Within

Source Speaks

Fall In Love with the Beloved Within

Source Speaks

by Chireya Fox

CODES OF UNION BOOK II

DIVINE LOVE WISDOM
PUBLICATIONS

Fall In Love with the Beloved Within

SOURCE SPEAKS

Codes of Union Companion Book to:
Unlocked and Unleashed: The God Within You • Amazon
Codes of Union: Divine Mother Speaks • Coming Soon

© Copyright 2017, Chireya Fox aka Laura C. Fox, Divine Love Wisdom Publications, All RightsReserved. No portion of this material may be duplicated in any form without express written permission of the author, with the exception of short quotes to be used to share wisdom and information about these writings.

ISBN 978-0-9907498-3-7

Download Free Guided Meditation Companion Audios at:
CHIREYA.COM/LOVE-BOOK

#chireyafox #loveyourselfmore #spiritualgrowth

TABLE OF CONTENTS

Foreword 17

Introduction 19

We Will Soar 27

Key Codes of Liberation 31

Your Resonance Barometer 35

Loyalty and Trust 39

Allowing the Qualities of Awareness
As Love to Guide Your Path 47

How Love Heals 71

Practice the Presence 77

Awareness of Love 81

Finding Love Within Yourself 87

Principles To Live By 101

Be In Love with the Beloved Within 107

Afterword – Are You the Mini Me of Source? 109

Stand Naked To The Truth—Poem 113

About The Author 115

To receive the exercises in this book as a free, printable PDF file, please scan the QR code below and/or visit:

CHIREYA.COM/LOVE-EXERCISES

THE DAY OF HOPE

The days of absence and the bitter nights
Of separation, all are at an end!
Where is the influence of the star that blights
My hope? The omen answers: At an end!
Autumn's abundance, creeping Autumn's mirth,
Are ended and forgot when o'er the earth
The wind of Spring with soft warm feet doth wend.

~ Hafiz

ACKNOWLEDGEMENTS

I would like to acknowledge writing coach Tom Bird, my dearly departed parents J. Christie and George Cruger; my brothers Daniel and Peter Cruger; my sons Benjamin and Zachary Fox; their dad Eric Fox and his wife Denise; my friends and champions of this work Rachel Prince, Doron Koutash, Rock Paliuca, Keith Michael Virgo, Kenneth Schwenker, Kweku Riverson, Sanjay Gupta, Kyra Storojev and Stephen Fantl; coach Vickie Gould; editor Kat Campise; trailer filmmakers Mikki Willis, Jerad Hobaugh, and Gabriel Valda; trailer actors Amber Brady and Ryan Mandell; e-book audio engineer Erik Lassi; foreword author Rev. Arlene C. Hylton; and web designer Pao Alcantara, all of whom have contributed to my ability to bring forth this book.
~ *Chireya*

DEDICATION

This book is dedicated to all the Master Teachers of love who know the Beloved Within and Bhakti Yogis who have graced this planet, known and unknown, including Shirdi Sai Baba, Ramana Maharshi, Papaji, Nityananda Bhagavan, Yogananda, Satchidananda, Buddha, Rumi, Hafiz, Jesus also known as Isa or Yeshua, and so many more.

I also dedicate this book to the beautiful teachers and "workers in the field" of our day who live by and share the principles of love, including my dear friends Tamber Bennett Zadawski, Robert Young, Doron Kutash, Nandhiji, Esther Hicks, Steve Adler, Alain Torres, Tony Robbins, Matt Kahn, Rhonda Lee, Dr. John Day and Coco, Athena Starseed, April Ree, Julian Forest, Justin Blackburn, Erik and Kelly Lawyer, Peter Cutler, Michael Perlin, Rev. Arlene Hylton, Kiana Prema, Brian Dickinson, Dr. Dream, Joanne Rees Ehlinger, Neil Gaur, Trevor Devol, Carol Fitzpatrick, Aubert Bastiat, David Seacord, and Kenneth Schwenker, and to my sons Ben and Zach who constantly teach me about love through their inspiring presence.

FOREWORD

AT YOUR FINGERTIPS you now have a mighty tool for self discovery, self realization, and self mastery. This book is an excellent gateway for readers to explore and recognize all that has hindered them from moving forward in their life. As each individual recognizes what has hindered them, and uses the simple yet transformative processes in this book, their life is changed for the Greater Good.

As my Spiritual Teacher Rev. Michael Bernard Beckwith says' You can be pushed by pain or pulled by a vision". This body of work written by Source through and as Chireya Fox supports you in being "Pulled by a vision". Vision happens when obstacles that have blocked us, such as self judgment, negative thinking, non-forgiveness etc., are healed and moved out of the way.

Your journey through these writings will help you unlock insights and a deeper understanding of your necessity in this gift called life. Your value will be evident as you recognize the potentiality within you. What Chireya teaches is not from a text book. It is from life experience, meditation and deep prayer with answers from Source. Her intuitive self is fully developed and supports her in guiding herself and others to the real understanding of Source or, as you will, the Higher

Self being the most powerful core of all individuals, and how it works as their Life. This is turn supports her in seeing the Divine in all human beings and guiding them to their own recognition of their Divinity. She is a powerful messenger of Source, and is an example of the creative power of Source active as her own being.

"Fall in Love with the Beloved Within" is an act of love. I consider the author to be a Master Teacher who not only teaches others but is teachable. Chireya's Life Mission is to support individuals in their healing so they may be a beneficial presence on the planet.

As you read the pages of this masterpiece and practice the process's, healing is eminent. Congratulations, on your yes to living a fulfilled Life, as you Fall in Love with the Beloved Within.

Blessings,

Rev. Arlene C. Hylton, Minister
Spiritual Teacher at Agape International Spiritual Center
Spiritual Director, Safe Harbor Treatment Center for Women

INTRODUCTION

REMEMBER THE EXHILARATION OF PLAY as a small child in the backyard? On the edge of expectancy, you felt light, vibrant—truly alive!

As people age, it is not that they no longer have access to that lightness of being. Instead, it is that they bought into the density of unloving thoughts and actions which in turn slowed them down, which eventually leads to a halt which we call death.

There are many other factors regarding the longevity of the human life stream, however, there is much more health, wealth, wisdom, power, knowledge, longevity, and well-being available to human beings than what they currently allow.

This book is a transmission from the highest levels of light. It is a gift from the Prime Source Creator, known by many names. This Source is the effulgent, effervescent, overflowing, divine presence of Life Itself – a perfect emanation of pure, Divine Love. This is the light and love of your True Self.

The pure perfect Divine Love and Light Source Creator is always present, all-powerful, and all-knowing. This is also called Omniscience, Omnipresence, and Omnipotence. The reason that this power is so all encompassing is because the Divine Source Creator is one hundred percent pure harmonic love. This love, without exception, blesses all things as they are — healing, recalibrating, and rejuvenating everyone and everything that comes into the Presence of it.

Love is a many splendored thing. Bask in it, bathe in it. Rekindle it daily. Caress it with your mind, and let it leap with joy in your heart. You are the awakening consciousness of love. That's why you feel so lonely when you think it is absent. Be full of yourself! Be full of love. That is the antidote. Immanence and Transcendence become One in this comprehension. The singularity within and behind everything and every one is the constant.

All things:

1. **Emerge from this Point of Oneness,**
2. **Flower (self-express), and**
3. **Return to the Void inside the Pre-Existent Unity, the Point of Oneness.**

From time immemorial the accolades have been sung to this One Source at the Center of All Creation, and spoken in multitudinous tongues from different Celestial Palaces and Planetary Spheres. On your own planet, the name is Source, God, Love. Many are the messengers of this One, whose Names have also been attributed with its qualities.

INTRODUCTION

Many are the Pathways that lead back Home to this One for the children who have emanated forth to experience the Glory of this Al Presence in myriad life streams.

Resting now upon the knowing that All Is Well, it is time to begin recalibrating to the Truth within you. You are not a mere mortal with a temporary existence, you are a vast interdimensional Aspect of the One. Since the beginning of time, you have gone forth to express this Love in myriad forms and yet in your current incarnation, you have forgotten who you are. The love and beauty of your body is deeper, richer, more powerful, more blissful and richer than you can possibly imagine from your current vantage point.

All that has gone before is but a flicker in time of your vast Being. As a Source Streaming Human Angel, you are the very embodiment of Love. There is nothing but goodness in you, and nothing but Choice that you must make.

As a Divine Chooser, your love soars into all probability fields assisting you in deciding which pathway will serve you best in any given moment. Your human garment is fettered with many chains of the past, making it more difficult to see and feel the Truth of you. It is through embracing the pain and suffering along with the joy and connection that you will be able to shed the layers of conditioning and pain, and awaken once more to the fullness of who you are.

A Subtle Human Energetic Program

There's a very subtle energetic program many human beings are running. It's an underlying feeling of "waiting for redemption," as if someone, some thing, some God or some experience will, one day, usher in the proof of our love-ability so that we can *finally* allow ourselves to love ourselves. This book is dedicated to bringing in a new comprehension, in all levels of the conscious and subconscious, in which we know that now we are already worthy of:

- All love
- All good things
- All joy
- All freedom
- All creative prowess
- All ability to contribute and be hear
- All positivity in loving relationships
- All prosperity and abundance
- All harmony
- All reflection of our purity and innate goodness from those around us

In this culture, we are typically trained to look outside of ourselves for approval. While many of us have shed deep layers of this conditioning, there still may be remnants of waiting for that approval from a mysterious unfathomable source. The waiting itself feels uncomfortable, and it's as though we are addicted to it. Ready to shed this layer? All we need to do is intend it to be so, and it will begin to clear out of our minds, bodies, souls, spirits, chakras, nadis, organs, tissues, glands, sinew, bones, bodily fluids, molecules, and cells. And so it is!

Stepping into Your Alignment

Your true identity is far beyond the human veil, yet your beautiful human nature and being is informed and sustained by this Light and this Love that you Are. The Mystery of the Singularity within you, contains the Truth of our Oneness with All That Is.

There is but One Light, there is but One Love, informing, animating and expressing as everything. And so if this is true, it must also be true that This Light Is You. Seek within to activate awareness of this Mystery within you, and all is well.

Each of us has a unique purpose which reflects to our original essence as a Spiritual Being. As a 'soul', we've had many incarnations, through which we built layers of experience, dharma, karma, trauma, skill, preference and so forth.

As we calibrate to our most aligned expression in this particular lifetime, there are levels and layers to shed, so we become clear channels of the vibrations which will ultimately be most satisfying to our spiritual nature.

Questions To Ponder

- Are you living your true divine purpose?
- Does it feel possible to do this while making a living?
- How committed are you to alignment on all levels?
- Does it feel risky to step into your full alignment?
- What would you have to give up?
- How willing are you to experience change right now, in order to live your life totally on purpose?

The energy with which and through which you create something new in your life is the energy which will reside within the manifestation.

No matter what the object of your creational intention is, the same rule of thumb applies for the manifestation. Be sure to be clear about what you desire, from a place of Joy, Peace and Harmony. In that way, your results will also be imprinted with these high vibrations.

I have 'dropped in' with Source in this book to bring forth the transmissions herein. They will take you deep into the Heart of Love and Truth, to reexamine life from a new perspective. When you emerge, you shall be able to answer the questions above from a whole new vantage point.

This is not just meant to be read as a mental exercise. To truly gain the shift you seek, you must actually embrace the doing part. The experiences you will have as a result of experiencing this book and its exercises will be unique to you. That's why I have created a complimentary .pdf

INTRODUCTION

file with the exercises to make it easy for you to print them out, as well as an Online Companion Course to the book, for those who want to dive deeper. I am also available for private coaching for those who desire more personalized attention in this empowering process.

Just keep opening to love—more and more love. The power of love itself will take care of any adjustments, with grace and in a loving way. It is not necessary to seek ego slaying. Life itself takes care of that. Sometimes, the perception of a need to slay the ego can be caught up with unworthiness. The needed medicine may be to love yourself more.

So enjoy it, take your time with it, play with it, and rest in the knowing that All is Well. I do look forward to hearing from you how this material serves you.

Should you feel inspired to dive deeper into this exploration with a guide, I am at your service. Many blessings on your path!

Love, Chireya

**Please visit Chireya.com/Love-Book
to discover more about private sessions, courses,
and programs related to this book, and to receive
complimentary guided meditations.**

WE WILL SOAR

This is Life.
The Teachings are here.
The Time is now.

LOOK NO FURTHER TO find the Gateway to the heart of pure love, for it is within you. The Keys in this book will unlock the Codes of Union within that have been lying dormant for eons, as you have cascaded as Soul through many earthly experiences.

Now is the time to unlock the codes and enter the gateway. You have reached the juncture on this planetary sphere some call graduation. It is also known as ascension or awakening.

Called by many names, there is one function in the Sequence of Beings, which culminates in this grand opening to the Heart of Love. It is a remembrance process, because though Love has never left you, your planetary consciousness attempted to explore that which is not love.

In the Grand Awakening of these Culminating Moments, you are cleaning out the closet of the past, reviewing your life, and deciding where to go from here, are you not?

So it is that this is natural and normal, perfect and beautiful—at this stage of the game. The Love that you are has always been with you. The fullness of its Purpose, Power and Presence, you have not as yet been able to fully grasp.

We know the times have been challenging, yet rest in the knowing that all is well, as the Grand Awakening is at hand.

You have done your homework. Some parts of this Curriculum have been easier than others. Yet here we are, setting the stage for a vast transformation the likes of which have not appeared for a very long time.

Rest in the knowing that All Is Well. Spirit — that which you may call God, Source, Love, Nature, Life — is within you, and is you. This is Truth.

When Truth is proclaimed, it cannot be denied. When Truth is felt, it opens new doors. When Truth is heard, it awakens the soul, and dismantles falsehoods masquerading as it. This is how Truth works. It does not beg, borrow or steal. It does not vilify, and it does not expire, neither does it clamor for attention or protest. Truth is as Truth does.

In this book, we will be revealing this Truth, and replacing ignorance with knowledge, fear with safety, and pity with comprehension.

Your self-worth is not in question, and never has been in the annals of time, the Book of Life. It is you who have judged yourselves, and thus experienced the consequences. The mechanics of this will be made plain, as you rest in the bosom of these Teachings. The Teachings and Teacher are within you. Tools like this book are here for just a little while longer, for only such time as you still require an outside reflection to comfort and reassure you.

In your multidimensional holographic nature, you already know these things. It is just that Consciousness has been sequestered in this domain in such a way as to cause temporary forgetfulness. We say to you that these times are coming to a close.

The grand nightmare of limitation, lack, fear, scarcity, shame, guilt, repression, anxiety, and feeling lost is reaching a culminating point. A chapter is ending. When you know that you know that you know that you are At One with the Source of All That Is, how can there be any fear?

When you can look out into the world and meet Love in the eyes of strangers, you will know you are home. When those who have hurt you in the past no longer cause an emotional charge to arise, you will know you are healed. When the wind whispers and you recognize yourself as one with it, you will know you are here.

Home. Healed. Here. One. Well. Present. Ineffable expanding love that knows no bounds. This is you.

This book is a gift, coming through a channel who has dedicated her life to the service of this Grand Awakening. Her love knows no bounds, and her core desire is to comfort you. The path of awakening has its challenges, and there have been challenges for her as well. Now, she is ready to deliver this message, as she has been preparing to do for a very long time. This is not about personality, this is not about attention, this is not about sacrifice. This is about a willingness to serve where help is needed.

Embrace the nature of your very own heart, which is Love. Simply let the words caress you, soothe you, remind you, and bless you, as piece by piece and one by one, the old constructs of delusion are dismantled. It is an easy process, though it may not always feel easy, as the old constructs of belief and thought that no longer serve you die away.

These old beliefs and constructs have taken on a semblance of reality, which is very convincing. Through the trickery of deceit, lies have been shared as truth. Through the Era of Deception, much suffering has occurred. The heart would seek peace, yet these constructs have masked the Truth the Heart would tell.

Well my beloved, now it is time to take off the mask. Now it is time to discover and uncover the Self. Now it is time to witness the Truth, and be embraced by it, to wash away the tears and the pain, once and for all.

—Source Speaks

We Love You

KEY CODES OF LIBERATION

**Facts are many,
but the truth is one.**
~ *Rabindranath Tagore*

THE RANTS OF THE MIND would ensnare you in self-pity and lack of self-worth. The mind rants from projections appearing real, and does not know where to turn for help.

Because the mind thinks that it is all there is, it cannot comprehend Oneness or Union. This is a snare that was set long ago, yet the villain has long been vanquished. But the prisoners do not know how to escape from this self-perpetuating prison.

This is why Teachings like this come to planets like yours.

When there is a need and a calling, Truth comes.

A need is a calling, in a vibrational way. When you have simply had enough of suffering, and the repetition of patterns, you cry out to the Universe for help, and help comes.

Your deep inner need to know Truth is a practical aspect of the self. There is a certain beautiful stubbornness to it, which shouts out to the Universe, "I will not be satisfied until I get to the bottom of this!" Even if this stubbornness shows up in ways that seem socially unacceptable, ways that perturb you or those around you, it is coming from a deep inner calling to cut through that which you call BS.

Your Inner Barometer knows no bounds, in attempting to synchronize with this Truth. Your tenacity may show up as depression. It may show up as a feeling of emptiness or concern.

It may show up as anger in the face of that which your vibrational intelligence knows beyond words is not true. Your vibrational intelligence is your BS Meter. Though you may not always know why you feel the way you do, your BS Meter is operating and steering you on subtle levels.

Hopefully this thought will help you make the decision to be less hard on yourself. You have been through a lot. You have been tricked. You have been fooled and cajoled by a false god consciousness which would rule in Love's place.

But never has there been a moment when the Spirit within you has bought into this false plan fully. Even if you succumbed and did things out of integrity with the Presence and Power of Love, there was always a part of you that grieved Love's perceived loss in that moment

Now, as the Awakening is at hand, Love is moving powerfully into focus as the Core of your Very Own Being.

Everywhere Present—Omnipresent
All Powerful—Omnipotent
All Knowing—Omniscient

This is Love. What unleashing the full Power and Presence will do for your world is beyond description. It is time now to unlock the Key Codes, which will set you free.

YOUR RESONANCE BAROMETER

YOUR BS METER HAS a mate. It is your RB, or Resonance Barometer. This means you can feel Love's Presence. You notice the feeling of being appreciated, the nice rush of comfort and ease when someone genuinely offers a smile, and the gentle touch of a helping hand reaching out in time of need.

These all make you feel good. When you feel good, you feel God. You feel Love. Love rushes in, with its blissful healing presence, to save the day at the last possible second!

Know that all is well. Love heals. This is Truth.

When situations and scenarios have reached a culmination point, in the seeming absence of love, worry and concern can take over. The very mechanism of this negative thought train actually compounds the situation and makes it seemingly worse.

This is quite the conundrum for the awakening soul, who may feel that no matter what, the situation keeps spiraling on a downward trajectory. Herein lies the Nature of the Law of Life. This is the First Key Code to be unlocked. You are Source.

CODE 1: YOU ARE SOURCE

As Source, the vibrations that emanate from you are Creative. In a world where fools have ruled and lies were crowned King, you were taught that "Life Happens to You." The single most important piece of information in the entire creation was kept from you. If you are wondering why chaos has triumphed—or seemingly has on this planet, you will now see the cause of it can be perfectly traced back to this one grand oversight.

When whom you call Jesus said, "The Kingdom of Heaven is Within You," and "Ye Are Gods," he was not joking! He was unveiling the Ever Present Truth. Those who objected to Truth's Presence for their own purposes, denied it, cajoled it, and made up lies to trick you into submission to their own agenda of control and domination. Now that the wool is being removed from your eyes, the Revelation is waiting ever presently, for your realization.

However, there are mechanics to this comprehension, because of the Grand Distortions that have been at play. To sort out the wheat from the chaff is to begin to dismantle the distortion and put reality back into a healthy perspective.

Perceiving The Truth

Perception has aspects. One is of the mind and one is of the heart, or knowing. Perceiving with the senses alone, or conjuring images birthed of thoughts resting on faulty towers, will only further convince one of the reality of untruths.

This is where the art of deception has been so powerful. In tangling up your mind into thoughts and beliefs based on the false agenda, your own inner mechanism of creation had been turned against you. This is why Prayer, intentional connection, attunement and alignment become paramount in sorting out the wheat from the chaff. Truth can be pointed to, but not forced upon you. It is not the nature of Truth to force anything. It is a gentle, unfolding process, which rallies the Love Cries to your senses, as one by one, you reinstate the Principles of Liberation into your being.

This Truth is like a seed. Once planted and watered, it can only grow into the fullness of its pattern. And so it is that you, a God Seed, will grow into the God Being that you are.

The Truth of You is undiminishable. Now, it is simply time to diminish your belief in that which is not you, so you can know the Truth of you fully, once again.

LOYALTY AND TRUST

TO WHOM ARE YOU LOYAL? Who do you trust? Do you find yourself awash in a sea of nebulous agreements and tentative reciprocity? From your current vantage point, notice that you wonder whether you are safe, sometimes even in your most cherished relationships. This has a two-fold reason.

1. Your BS Meter can detect off-vibrations, even when your conscious mind can't. You can sense if someone has your best interest in mind, or not, even if you are not aware of what they are saying or doing behind your back.

2. Your own inner programming itself may have caused you to mistrust others, because of experiences in this lifetime or others, and because of any conditioning from your relatives and ancestors.

So now you can see the conundrum, which will also help you comprehend why you doubt yourself sometimes, and why it is sometimes hard to trust yourself with others. This is a gnarly knot to untangle, and yet the great untangling has begun. You must learn to sort out the wheat from the chaff. The wheat and the chaff exist in your own mind and being. Which thought is helpful, which impulse will lead towards Love's doorway, and which will lead down a darker path where it is more difficult to feel Love's Presence?

There is a mechanism in you, which can help bypass the superstition and conditioning of the mind.

It takes practice and training to get fully on board with this mechanism under the current circumstances, yet the mechanism itself is intrinsic to your True Divine Nature, so ultimately, it can't be tampered with. It can only be temporarily blocked from view. Your Spirit is too strong to acquiesce to falsehoods, doubt and confusion forever.

CODE TWO: UNLOCKING: THE MASTERY OF YOUR MIND AND AWARENESS

It is not enough to only know the Truth. You must also master the awareness of it at all times. Do not be frightened by that statement. It is a given that permanent Mastery of Awareness is a goal to be attained, and you are not wrong if you do not already possess it.

Let's contemplate awareness for a moment. What is it? Perhaps we can comprehend it better by considering what it is not.

1. It is not a thing. It is not a concept. It is not a construct.
2. It's not an experience, though it can be experienced.
3. It does not have a beginning or an end, neither does it have plot points or culmination sequences. It is not for sale; you cannot rent it.
4. You cannot borrow or steal it from another, yet you can bask in it together.
5. It is not something you can forget or remember, though you can diminish your awareness of it through distraction.

We also may not be able to put our finger on exactly *what* it is. Yet, we can examine its qualities.

1. It is ineffable.
2. It is ever-present.
3. It is all-knowing.
4. We may not be able to feel Its all-pervasive power in regular walking moments, yet we can determine that if it is ever-present and all-knowing, it must also contain some secret power.
5. It is calm and gentle, like a clear lake. It is smooth and reliable, like your favorite lover. It is mysterious, and it is simple all at once.
6. We cannot escape from it, nor would we want to.

If we put two and two together through this contemplation, we begin to illuminate the fact that Awareness is very much like what we call God or Source or Love. And, the fact that we can't escape from it in our conscious living state would also indicate that it either *is* or is *intrinsically intertwined with* our very own nature.

Are we this awareness which we seek to comprehend? If this awareness is in fact our very own nature, and it is simultaneously like the Source of All That Is, some call God, now we can begin to puzzle out the possibility, that we may in fact, be At One with this Source-God, which is Love.

We Are Love.

- **What is the underlying platform upon which this Awareness rests?**

In contemplating the Nature of this Awareness, we can easily see that it rests upon itself. While it has a floating quality, it is neither floating nor stationary. The essence of Its omnipresence dictates it cannot be up or down, it cannot be behind us or in front of us, and it cannot be slow or fast.

Awareness *is*. This is the great Business of 'Isness'. The *IS* is, existing as the foundation behind the Generative Capacity of Nature. Let's examine the word 'IS', made up by the line and the spiral. Place them together and they become the symbol of the currency of a nation, $. They resemble the double helix running up the spine, as expressed in the traditions of Yoga. This is pointing to the lifeblood or currency of creation—or 'Isness'. This is remarked upon by leading physicists of your world as the Background Energy of Creation. Many scientists are discovering through your regular scientific means that this Background Energy is inexhaustible. It is endless, eternal, effulgent, and overflowing—everywhere present, divine, and always there.

From tapping the background energy of creation, many great scientists of your time and before have discovered a way to create an inexhaustible supply of energy to power human creations. Yet for some time, the technologies which allow this energy to come forth for free have been suppressed. Make no mistake about it—there is a great correspondence here between the suppression of these advanced energy technologies which create a limitless supply and the repression of the information that you are in fact at one with the eternally flowing and abundant Love and Power.

If people were to discover the one, surely they would uncover the other, and the game of deception would soon be over. Millions of beings realizing they are One with the Power of the Universe, and that the Love, the omnipresent Substance of the Universe is their True Nature, would no longer be controllable, would they? It should now become apparent why the mastery of this awareness is instrumental to unlocking the Truth of Who You Are, and setting yourself free.

Dismantling the layers of false beliefs covering the Truth of You, now becomes tantamount to freeing the world from the confines of suffering, and even death. If we contemplate this Awareness further, we can reason and eventually experience that death does not knock on Its door. Eternal, ineffable Suchness, pure awareness, is the Ground of Being—all Being, here, now, there, and then.

EXERCISE 1: MAKE THE CONNECTION

Rest in the knowing that All Is Well. Close your eyes, take a deep breath, and simply allow your mind to rest upon this Ineffable Suchness called awareness. The length of this contemplation doesn't matter as long as you simply make the connection.

EXERCISE 2: FEEL THE REALNESS

Write down your thoughts and feelings about the experience of connecting with Awareness. Did it feel difficult or easy? Were you distracted? Was there a moment of insight?

EXERCISE 3: WITNESS YOURSELF

Now, stand in front of a mirror. Simply witness yourself. Take a look. Who's there?

Then, write your experience in your journal.

NOTE: It is recommended to dedicate a journal to writing out the exercises in this book.

You may also wish to download a complimentary, printable .pdf version of the exercises at Chireya.com/love-exercises to help you in your process.

For a complimentary guided meditation related to this chapter, called **Learning To Trust Love,** *please visit Chireya.com/love-book.*

ALLOWING THE QUALITIES OF AWARENESS AS LOVE TO GUIDE YOUR PATH

> **And the walls come tumbling down.**
> ~ *The Style Council*

WHAT ARE THE QUALITIES of this Awareness?

**Simple • Mysterious • Ever-present
Non-alarming • Restful • Peaceful • Steady
Open • Awake • Witnessing**

From these qualities, we can derive and further understand the reasoning behind the universal spiritual teachings of Love.

- We can see that this awareness is non-judgmental by nature. We can see that it is unconditional in its expression, which feels like Love.
- We can even see how the concept of non-attachment is related to this mysterious, ever-present awareness, witnessing all and loving all as it is—holding All That Is in its eternal embrace.

- We can feel a complete lack of resistance in its essence.

These teachings of non-attachment, unconditional love, non-judgment and non-resistance can fascinatingly be found in all the major spiritual systems' as Tenets, Practices, and Understandings.

We can see that the root and core of these traditions have come from the same Source—a loving Source that has never abandoned anyone, and that is always there, no matter what.

It now becomes easy to detect any fallacies, lies, and distortions of religious systems. Any place where a system would cast judgment or blame, make hate sacred, or clutch onto people or circumstances enforcing conformity, this would be the opposite of the very truths at the foundation of these systems.

Teachings of Love

Non-judgment • Unconditional Love
Non-attachment • Non-resistance

At first glance, these teachings may feel like misplaced lunacy or spiritual fluff. A connotation of Goodie Two Shoes-ness may surface, and it may feel more comfortable to push aside these ideas, and replace them with notions of "the real world."

"The real world does not operate on unconditional love," you may say. "It operates on conditional love and fear of scarcity." Judgment, division, and separation exist as tenets which keep this "real world" in place. If we go beyond the delusion of lack, limitation, scarcity, separation, judgment, condemnation, arrogance, and blame, the world itself would not continue to exist in the way it does now. It would simply cease to be.

What if the world of hatred and fear needed your attention—your Awareness—in order to exist? If this Awareness is in fact the All Powerful Background Energy of the Universe, then doesn't it make sense that where it flows, there the power goes?

What would happen to this flickering projection of a fearful world if you were no longer feeding it your Awareness through your Attention? Answer: the all powerful 'something-ness' would go to work building what you shift your attention to.

Attention = The Door Man
Awareness = The Door

Let's examine these teachings of love, one by one.

Unconditional Love

Unconditional Love is the foundation of All That Is. Imagine a world where the Creator had gone mad, and didn't love their creation. This would be chaos indeed. This is the world we have conjured up with our minds, yet the good news is this is not the underlying truth of the matter. By our own inner power, we have, knowingly or unknowingly, crystallized thought forms through which the divine energy flows. These thought forms appear as the mind stuff we generated. This is how it came to be that we could have an experience of lack, limitation, fear, and scarcity, from eons of such thinking.

In other words, the unconditionally loving Nature of the Prime Creator allows all. This Prime Creator has endowed us with the attributes of creation—thought, word, feeling and deed. All these cause vibrations to pulse outward, attracting more vibrations like themselves, resulting in an appearance that magnetizes into our own experience of reality.

The Universe is made of Thought Stuff. When the little Creators, us, let our own thoughts run rampant without monitoring our own BS Meter, we created negative thought forms that lead to unpleasant results. Once this occurs, we then reflect upon those thought forms, further attracting similar thoughts and experiences. This "compounded momentum" continues to cascade and crescendo as we struggle to make sense of what is happening to us in our world.

Since the Teachings had been hidden and lost, the people did not know, this is how life works. Therefore, they did not know how to recalibrate and change trajectory. This, as you can imagine, happened for eons, putting the human race on your planet in the awkward position of not knowing from whence it came, or how to course correct when things got out of hand. It just seems like things keep getting worse, and we wonder if we are being punished, or if there are dark forces out to get us.

The truth is, vibrations of lower than love attract the same, so beings were attracted who matched these lower density frequencies the human race was emanating. Then began the game of domination and control in an amnesiac world. Thus the cycles compounded further and much suffering has been experienced. We say, "has been experienced," on purpose. While everything is made of thought forms and is thus transient and ever changing, the experience of suffering has been a reality for you.

Unconditional Love says, no matter what has transpired, no matter what has occurred, you are loved. You are the very nature of love, absent minded as you may be to this reality at any given moment. There are no holds barred in Love's embrace. Love loves you, even when you can't. The vast amount of energy poured into thought forms that led to negative results powered the grid of a negative dream.

Now that you, the dreamer, are awakening, you will be able to recalibrate to the Truth of You relatively quickly. Unconditional Love is your Primary Tool to do this with. When Loving All That Is as It Is, you are "being like" the Prime Creator, Source, which also means, you are being yourself.

When you are being yourself, Truth is present, because you are in that moment experientially beholden to the Truth of You. Do you see the physics of it? Do you see the simplicity? Surely, the way out of hell is more simple than we could have imagined, though its gates may have appeared closed securely all around us.

Now is the time on this planetary sphere where the shackles of pain and suffering through the belief in Love's absence will be dismantled and undone for good. Now is the time of your awakening to Unconditional Love. Now is the time of the Great Return—to sanity, to sanctity, and to the consciousness which knows love is real.

Only Love Is Real
~ MC Yogi

UNCONDITIONAL LOVE PRACTICE SESSION

EXERCISE 4: LOVE YOURSELF

Rest in the knowing that all is well, as you make the intention to allow Love's Presence back into your life. What comes up for you, as you contemplate unconditionally loving yourself?

Are there parts of you that are scared you don't deserve this love? Embrace them. Love them.

Let those parts know, whatever has transpired, whatever you have done, whenever others have judged you as guilty or wrong, none of these things can ever take away the Truth that you are Loved absolutely. What would it feel like if this were true? Do emotions arise? Let them.

EXERCISE 5: EXTEND LOVE

Imagine someone you really don't like, or who did something you are still resentful about. Ask yourself, what would it be like if you could shower them with love anyway? What would it feel like to you to open your heart and extend love, even if it feels like they don't deserve it? Even if just for a moment, see if you can open your heart and extend love to this person. Notice what happens to you, inside of you, as you do this. Do you feel better? Do you feel more peaceful? Do you feel Love? This is the Key—the Master Key — that unlocks all doors. From here it is plain to see that it is not what another does, but what *you* do that determines whether or not you can feel love's presence. **Write out your experience of Unconditional Love in your journal now.**

Non-Judgment

Why is it that the Great Masters say not to judge one another? Could it be that our discoveries around Unconditional Love have something to do with this? If the quality of your experience directly relates to what you are putting out, rather than what others are sending to you, then it makes sense and becomes sheer logic that to judge another would be to unwittingly cast a spell of "not good enough" upon yourself. Notice the difference in how you feel when you judge someone, and when you send love to someone, even if they did something you did not like. Remember, this is a vibrational Universe. That which emanates from you, returns to you.

Love Your Enemies
~ Jesus

Instantaneously, you feel the results of your own thought projections. You may think you are simply being wise and knowing more than others by pointing out their faults, labeling them or otherwise negatively assessing their character.

But the truth is, as you do this, you condemn yourself in that moment to a natural cascade of returning flow of the same nature.

This is why you don't feel good when talking about what they've done or how they haven't lived up with the goodness you sought in them. The distaste in your mouth is coming not from them, but from your own thoughts about them. It's coming from you judging them! You have set your own thought mechanism into motion in a negative direction. This is what makes you feel bad, every time.

Instant Karma's Gonna Get You
~ John Lennon

This may feel like a harsh disclosure, or sheer nonsense. But the good news is, you have the capacity to turn the energy around in the blink of an eye. In leveraging the power of your own consciousness, you can shift how you feel instantaneously, by directing your thoughts towards love.

Even if you don't think they deserve it, your Inner Awareness knows, they too are just like you—At One with the great Creative Force behind all life. They too are unconditionally loved by the Source, just like you, even when they have caused themselves suffering by not knowing these things and being out of rhythm with Love.

Do you choose to be the Great Condemner, thereby condemning yourself to similar vibrations? Or would you prefer to be the Great Witness, loving and embracing all that is as it is, and reaping the benefits in your very own consciousness?

NON-JUDGMENT PRACTICE SESSION

EXERCISE 6: OVERCOMING JUDGMENT 1

One by one, bring up in your mind three or four people whom you don't like or who have hurt you in some way.

- Notice your thoughts about them. How do you feel when contemplating them?
- What can you tell from what you are feeling; about the nature of the results you would get from this feeling?

- Are you able to hold a steady stream of unconditional love for them, or does your mind wander to negativity making you feel bad?

Write out your notes about this process in your journal now.

Practice makes perfect! As you calibrate more and more to the Truth of You, which is Love, it will become easier and easier to Return To Love, moment by moment, day by day.

Remember—Love is not judging you for not having mastered this yet. Will you judge yourself?

Love is a many splendored thing.
~ Paul Francis Webster

EXERCISE 7: OVERCOMING JUDGMENT 2

- Make a list of the 10 things or people you hate or dislike most.
- Next to each one, write on a scale of one to ten, how willing you are to become unconditionally loving towards them?
- Starting with the easiest one first, practice opening your heart to love as you envision this person, situation or thing melting in this love.
- Imagine a stream of beautiful Pink Light emanating from your heart, and filling the space

around them. (They can receive it or not on the inner planes, as they wish.)
- Notice how the person, place or thing changes form, begins to smile, or disappears right before your eyes. Notice how you feel.
- Now, go onto the next most easy to love item, and repeat the process until you have experienced the dynamic healing release of Unconditional Love for each of them. It will become easier to do this with the higher numbers, once you have practiced with the easier ones.
- Write how this exercise was for you.
- Did it bring up emotions or anxiety?
- Did you gain any insight?

Non-Attachment

If Love does not judge, neither does it bind. The mind shall be caressed with this Love, until it becomes willing to let go of people, places, situations, and things. "Letting" is another word for "giving birth." When we let go, we allow people, places, and circumstances to be what they will be. When we cling to notions of how we feel they ought to be, we bind ourselves to them in a negative, "attached" way, causing more suffering for ourselves and others.

To love someone and desire to be with them, and love having them in your life, is different from being attached.

When you do this with an open heart, and an awareness of their freedom to choose, you are being "like Love," and loving them unconditionally. On the contrary, to be attached is to deny Love's Presence. It is as if you are saying, "I need this person, place or thing to be a certain way so I can be safe, and so I can love them." In that moment, you are unaware of Love's ever present nature.

When you are not aware of Love's ever present nature, you are in that moment coming from fear, and attempting to latch onto outer circumstances or people in a vain attempt to find love and comfort outside of yourself.

Does this mean you will be abandoned, if you allow yourself to detach from needing something or someone to be a certain way? Not necessarily. But remember that this phenomenal world is ever-changing, and there is ultimately nothing permanent to latch onto. This is one of the hardest lessons for most human beings to learn, and there are complex and long-term reasons why this is so. In this book, we are taking you step by step into the comprehension of those things so you can be free.

Non-attachment does not mean you cannot have a beneficial influence on people. You can! And, just imagine how good it feels when someone accepts you just the way you are, and loves you right here and right now, no matter what.

Recall a moment when someone deeply listened to you, and did not try to change you.

Did that feel liberating? Were you able to more easily make any needed changes in that space of Love?

Each person desires to have goodness, beauty, peace, prosperity, well-being and an opportunity to share. This is part of their divine blueprint. When we love what is, without resistance, we are allowing this power of love to sort things out. The person can then make a better choice, from their own free will, in their own divine timing. Then, you can shift your attention to something more appealing to you, thereby generating more of that in your experience.

Questions that may arise as you contemplate non-attachment:

- If I let go, will I be abandoned?
- What if I really know what's best for this person or circumstance? And if I can't make them listen and do it my way, what if they will suffer as a result?
- What if I'm married to someone or have kids? How is this idea of non-attachment even possible?
- Won't others feel I am abandoning them if I detach and let go?
- What is the difference between aloofness and attachment?
- How do I tell if I'm being aloof or practicing non-attachment?

- How do I let go when I'm really, really attached, and it's difficult for me to do so emotionally?
- How does non-attachment relate to my own perception and feelings about myself?
- How can Love help me feel my own inner power, as I sort out this energy of attachment in my life?

Write out any more questions that arise for you. Trust that Life Itself will bring you the answers, through this book or other life experiences.

THE FOLLOWING ARE RESPONSES FROM SOURCE'S LOVING PERSPECTIVE:

- **If I let go, will I be abandoned?**

You are never abandoned by Love! People have their own free will. Some will stay in your life, and some will move on. People may come and go.

When someone departs your life, see if you can find the gift in this transition.

Is it opening you to a new set of possibilities?

What did you appreciate about the person who left?

- **What if I really know what's best for this person or circumstance? And if I can't make them listen and do it my way, what if they will suffer as a result?**

(See following response in regards to children or dependents).

If you feel you know what is best for someone, and they have not asked for this advice, then you can imagine the best for them in your own mind and heart. Visualize them being happy and learning all they need to learn, to fully express themselves in this life. Turn it over to God-Source-Love. Bring them to this Source, imagine them begin received and bathed in Love, and finding a way to take the next perfect step on their path.

If they are really in trouble, tune in with Source deeply and ask Source how you may best help them. You will receive an answer if you wait for the still small voice. Also, there are many prayer groups such as Silent Unity, that can also help add positive energy to their lives.

First and foremost, deal with the emotional charge and grief or anger within you, as it relates to them. When you can collapse that and heal your attachment to them being a certain way, you will more readily be guided to assist them in a truly effective way.

- **What if I'm married to someone or have kids? How is this idea of non-attachment even possible?**

When you've chosen to have someone in your life, by marrying them or giving birth to them or in other circumstances, they are there for a reason.

Many times, family members have come together for the purpose of helping each other learn life's lessons. When difficulties arise, or when you notice you or others are seriously attached to someone in the family being a certain way, this is an opportunity to love them more, love yourself more, and practice this spiritual lesson of non-attachment.

It doesn't mean you have to leave them! It just means you get to practice letting them be themselves and make their own choices.

Obviously, as the parent of a small child, you will intervene if they are in harm's way. Having small children or even older children may be one of the most challenging circumstances under which to learn this law of non-attachment. But the rewards will be great. Any time you *can* allow them to make their own choices, to feel their own desires, and to express themselves, you will be breaking bonds and fetters that had been cemented in your ancestral lineage and past lives through eons.

- **Won't others feel I am abandoning them if I detach and let go?**

It depends how you are doing it. If you are being aloof, you are not really practicing non-attachment.

They might actually feel even more loved, and desire to be around you more, if you practice non-attachment in a way in which they feel the loving presence of your acceptance of them, just as they are.

- **What is the difference between aloofness and attachment?**

Aloofness has a negative, "passive aggressive" quality to it. Non-attachment as we're discussing it here has a loving and gentle quality to it. It is the space of "allowing." It is a space of unconditional love.

Aloofness means, "I'm ignoring you because you're not really behaving the way I want, and I'm trying not to care that this bothers me, and I don't want to admit that I want you to suffer a bit because you are not letting me control you."

Non-attachment as we are using it here means, "I love that you are *you*, and I love your being. I trust the Divine to help you express life just the way *you* are meant to, and I'll sit back and watch, and marvel at the genius that is you! If you ever desire my help, insight or reflection, I'm more than happy to offer it! Just ask!"

- **How do I tell if I'm being aloof or practicing non-attachment?**

If you are being aloof, your BS Meter will detect a subtle or not so subtle negative feeling inside of you. Your love for others will decrease, not increase. If you are practicing non-attachment, you will feel present, centered, and safe, and you will feel the presence of Love. You may even feel joy, relief, or exhilaration in the state of non-attachment. Your love for others will increase, not decrease.

- **How do I let go when I'm really, really attached, and it's difficult for me to do so, emotionally?**

First of all, return to our lessons on Unconditional Love. Practice loving yourself unconditionally, even with this attachment. Practice non-judgment, with yourself as the subject. This is a wisdom teaching, not another excuse for you to beat yourself up.

Do not be attached to non-attachment!
~ Puppetji

- **How does non-attachment relate to my own perception and feelings about myself?**

When you are lovingly non-attached to needing yourself to be a certain way, likewise, you will find that you are more easily able to make healthy changes in your life.

Let's say you've always judged yourself for being too fat, or not smart enough, or not having enough money, or not being in a relationship, or not attracting the best partners. Whatever it is that bugs you about you, what would it take to love yourself anyway, and let go of any attachment to when this situation will shift or change?

The state of non-attachment is the state of allowing. When you are there, you will feel more peaceful, and new ideas of how to move things in the directions of your desires will begin to come to you naturally. This takes practice. That's why we're writing this book. See if you can let go of attachment to being hard on yourself when you haven't manifested all you desire just yet.

How can Love help me feel my own inner power, as I sort out this energy of attachment in my life? When you embark upon the journey to true, unconditionally loving non-attachment, you are setting forth to change the way you think at a core level. Appreciate yourself for embarking on this journey.

Humanity has been practicing attachment and conditional love for many, many eons! You are breaking a very old mold as you step onto this path.

Love sees you and respects your decision. Know that all is well, as you realize this is a process. You will learn and integrate each day, through experiences that arise. Acknowledge and appreciate yourself, for doing something bold. Acknowledge yourself with each triumph, and use each setback as an excuse to love yourself more. The reason why attachment in the negative sense has become so rampant on this planet comes from the same place as the belief that judging others will make us safe.

The energy is turned around and backwards from the Truth of You—but once again, as you reflect on these things, and notice places where you may have been experiencing attachment, this is not an opportunity to judge yourself for it. Again, it is an opportunity for you to love yourself more, and to simply notice what is transpiring in your consciousness. Be the witness to your own attachments and set yourself free!

This is a process. It took a while for humanity to

get here, to a place of judgment, attachment, resistance and a perception of Love's absence.

It will take practice and diligence to master the mind, for the purpose of overcoming its faulty beliefs and mis-perception.

Love's power, once activated, will go to work to quickly call your attention to any place where you cannot see or feel love.

This is truly an awareness game, and one in which there are legions standing by to assist you at every turn on the inner planes of Life.

Non-Resistance

> **Nothing can resist a truly non-resistance being.**
> *~ Lao Tse*

This section culminates in the teaching of Non-Resistance. First, we must explore the nature of resistance itself, in order to fully embrace a distinction in how to live from non-resistance.

resistance: noun

1. the act or power of resisting, opposing, or withstanding.
2. the opposition offered by one thing, force, etc., to another.

3. *Electricity.*

   a. Also called ohmic resistance. A property of a conductor by virtue of which the passage of current is opposed, causing electric energy to be transformed into heat: equal to the voltage across the conductor divided by the current flowing in the conductor: usually measured in ohms.

   b. a conductor or coil offering such opposition; resistor.

4. *Psychiatry.* opposition to an attempt to bring repressed thoughts or feelings into consciousness.

"What you resist persists"
~ Modern Saying

"What Is" is cascading to you, as a constant flow of experience, interaction, and circumstances. How have these experiences, interactions, and circumstances culminated in this way?

They have come about through the self-same mechanism of the Law of Life—"that which goes around, comes around."

To resist "what is" is to push against, make wrong, or deny your very own creation. As an Aspect of Source, your consciousness is creative and brings forth experience. If you do not like the experience that has arisen in your life, that is, of course, okay. Are you going to be able to change it, though, by pushing against it, making it wrong, or denying it? If you recognize the Truths revealed in this book so far, you'll see that by pushing against something, making it wrong, or denying it, you are once again filtering your own Divine Source Energy through a negative filter, and the only consequence by nature is for more negative streams to boomerang back into your own experience.

Do you see the light in this? It is sheer logic. Spirituality now becomes in our own comprehension, what it has always been—physics! Welcome to the metaphysics of reality and the mechanics of "how it works."

You are starting to comprehend more now, yes?

There are complexities to this scenario which are addressed further in the first book of the series, *"Unlocked and Unleashed: The God Within You– Divine Father Speaks"*. For example, how is it possible to be unconditionally loving, non-judgmental, and non-resistant to really bad stuff?

Just allow your mind to know that we are guiding you step by step in this Codes of Union series into the comprehension of these things. If you feel you really need to address these complexities now, we recommend reading *"Unlocked and Unleashed: The God Within You– Divine Father Speaks"*.

Your Tools

- **Non-Resistance**

- **Non-Attachment**
- **Non-Judgment**
- **Unconditional Love**

Just like with any tool, it takes practice to use it. Most importantly, practice utilizing these tools on yourself. Contemplate these things, and know that all is well.

- Can you love yourself unconditionally, just the way you are, right now, just as Source does?
- Can you stop judging yourself and making yourself feel wrong for the way you are?
- Can you let go of attachment? Of needing yourself to be a certain way?
- Can you cease resisting your life the way it is and open your heart to *loving you*, no matter what?

For a complimentary guided meditation related to this chapter, called **Activate Higher Awareness In A Busy Life***, please visit Chireya.com/love-book.*

HOW LOVE HEALS

THE POWER AND PRESENCE OF LOVE as the background of all creation has the properties of non-resistance, unconditional love, non-attachment, and non-judgment already built into it. Thus it is also intrinsically an energy of healing, as any sore spots of tension or pain can be washed away.

Tension, pain, anxiety, fear, sadness, grief, loss, blame, shame, hatred, anger, envy, and all emotions we call negative, have as their foundational cause a perception of a lack of love. It is that simple, even though the creation as it stands seems so complex.

The conditioning of our worldly experiences has engendered, over time, a belief in the lack of love leading to these emotions. As we emerge from the womb and drop into life on Earth, we witness these types of patterns already existing in the people around us.

By nature of the mechanism of the Law of Life, also known as the Law of Attraction, we begin immediately to innocently emulate the thought patterns of those around us. This self-perpetuating mechanism of continuation through conditioning of the culture results in what we call compounded momentum. This compounded momentum is backed by thoughts and beliefs flavored with a variety of vibrational densities, depending on the flavor of the thought stuff activating it.

In layman's terms, what goes around comes around! If you continue to think like your ancestors and relatives, you will continue to get similar results in life.

This is where practice and diligence are paramount, because often, this cultural conditioning is normal for us. Thus it exists beyond acute awareness in the realm of fuzzy ever-presence which we don't question, simply because it has been there so long! In order to heal, or change a circumstance or relationship, we have to let go of our beliefs defining "what is."

In order to let go of beliefs defining "what is," we need to allow love to penetrate our minds and bodies, allowing love to gracefully change things back to their natural state.

What is this natural state? The Power and Presence of Love Itself is our natural state. Thus, anything unlike Love will be recalibrated back to the essence underlying it. This means the fears, beliefs, and thought forms unlike love are up for deletion from our systems. As these non-loving thoughts and patterns of belief are deleted from our consciousness, our set point changes, and so does our world, in time.

The world is a giant biofeedback machine. If you've ever suspected that maybe you are living in a cosmic video game, all we can say is, the analogy is a good one!

The compounded momentum of lower density thought streams has caused a smoke screen to cover our perception of reality. The culmination of eons of collective compounded momentum has created appearances of chaos leading to the mistrust of life itself, and mistrust of God, or Source. If Source and Love were real, how could these painful things have come to be?

The loving heart cannot help but ask these questions. When we say "consciousness is an inside job," we are not kidding. As your consciousness changes, literally, the world changes with you.

As an extension of Source, you also are an extension of the World. Your awareness and attention are the mechanisms through which the world gets its operating budget—energetically. Think of your consciousness as the grid powering the world. How then can the world help but change, as you pull your attention from those displeasing manifestations, and begin to power up the new grid of Loving Kindness, envisioning and "voting with your vibration" for a new platform of reality based on love?

Vote with Your Vibes
~ Chireya

Every time you place your awareness in a certain direction, you are in fact, voting with your vibes. This is an act of the awareness of Love, and this is how Love Heals. Love heals through you and your very own leveled up consciousness!

> **There is only One Presence, One Power, and One Being, active in my life and in the Universe, God the Good, Omnipotent.**
> ~*The Unity Prayer*

The new pattern based on your new thoughts may appear to have some lag time before "kicking in" and showing up in your reality. This is where trust comes in! Once you have seen this Action of the Law in operation, you can come to rely on it consciously more and more. We have all heard the saying, "As a man thinketh, so is he." This is Law.

To get ourselves unstuck from the rut of past thinking, we must naturally start creating a new rivulet in the other direction.

This is where the processes of affirmations, intentions, prayer, meditation, declaration, and envisioning come in handy. These are redirection tools that will help you get from where you are to where you want to go.

For the novice who is just beginning to practice these things, these are the initiating tools to carve out a new probability stream for your life. For the more advanced student of life, these are the creational tools that help you further define and develop your dreams and set them into motion.

> **Never give up on yourself.**
> ~ *Master K*

Remember, practice makes perfect! It took you a while to get where you are now. When the Power of Love and directed thought kicks in, your shifts will take less time than the time it took to create the pattern.

There are many tools and practices, systems and modalities, that are on the forefront of the consciousness movement. Tune in and seek out those like-minded people, places, and practices which can help you get from where you are now, to where you want to go. Work it, baby!

It works when you work it!
~ Chireya

PRACTICE THE PRESENCE

What would love do?

IN OUR EMERGING SPIRITUAL MATURITY, we know that Practice Makes Perfect. This applies to worldly endeavors as well as to the inner technologies of the Presence. Presence with a capital "P" indicates the Presence of Love—the background energy of the Universe.

When learning to ride a bike, we eagerly watched the older kids get on and go. This may have caused some consternation because we couldn't do it yet, but it also caused our processor, the mind, to automatically begin to imagine ourselves riding that bike.

Depending on the intensity of the desire, and our general readiness for the task, a time sequence for actually owning the bike riding skill was set in motion.

In this case, the Presence of Love Itself is the big kid on the block. As we ask ourselves what love would do, we leverage this Presence as our Primordial Mentor. Likewise, there are those human beings in plenty who seem to be one or two steps ahead of us, in terms of benevolently being able to hold themselves in alignment with this Presence. These beings too, become our mentors, role models and elder siblings—the big kids. We can lovingly and playfully invite in the Spirit of any being whom we wish to claim as mentor and role model. Maybe this is someone in your life, a truly loving grandparent, or a kind neighbor. Maybe you saw someone in the grocery store who radiated so much love with just a simple smile that you chose to adopt them into your inner fleet of Love Teachers.

There are those beings we know such as Jesus, who embraced the God Within for all to see and bear witness to, and Buddha, whose great dharmic principles embody the truth of these things, giving us a set of eternal tools to set us free. Perhaps a Mother Teresa or a Gandhi or a Martin Luther King comes to mind—or someone like John Lennon.

While every human being here on the physical plane still has work to do and is still opening towards this total God Realization in one way or another, they may be one step ahead of us, and therefore, offer a living example of how to overcome the old conditioning towards attachment, judgment, resistance and a seeming lack of love.

Mentoring has long been known as the single most powerful way to learn a new skill. This is because when you are immersed in and surrounded by thought forms of a certain kind, it is much easier for you to tune your vibrations to the level of your mentor's thought forms. This works both ways—and as we were conditioned by our parents, siblings and relatives unconsciously at a young age, now we can consciously choose our mentors, and know that the fruit of our practiced Presence will ripen for the plucking, by nature

EXERCISE 8: SPIRITUAL ROLE MODELS 1

Let's imagine several scenarios in which we might need such modeling.

- Someone cuts in line at the grocery store. What would Mother Theresa do?
- Your spouse or partner reacts angrily to a situation he or she wanted to be different.
  What would Buddha do?
- A terrible thing occurs on the news and you feel impacted by it.
  What would Jesus do?
- You experience a loss of some kind. What would an enlightened sage do?

EXERCISE 9: SPIRITUAL ROLE MODELS 2

Imagine the patience and wisdom of the Dalai Lama, bearing the fruit of compounded momentum for an entire lineage and country. How do you imagine he holds himself with such grace, even under disastrous circumstances? **Write your responses in your journal now.**

EXERCISE 10: SPIRITUAL ROLE MODELS 3

Who are some of your favorite role models, either famous or from your personal life? List them in your journal, and note the characteristics you would like to model.

Now, take your responses from exercises 1, 2 and 3, and turn them into a list of Qualities you feel are aligned with Practicing the Presence. Turn these Qualities into a list of affirmations for yourself: Start each affirmation with the declaration, I AM. **Write them in your journal now.**

As you claim this life skill of Practicing the Presence, doors will open to you to show you the way into deeper levels of mentorship with the Power and Presence of Love. Many beings, situations, and circumstances will arise as Love's Agents, to take you on to the next steps of your Heart Centered Curriculum.

EXERCISE 11: OVERCOMING REACTIVITY

Write in your journal now, four characteristics you now choose to develop after reading this chapter and doing the first 3 exercises. The simple act of writing these down will set the wheels in motion. You are on your way. Remember, your attention is powerful, and is the driver to your adventure in reality.

AWARENESS OF LOVE

EVERY TIME YOU PLACE YOUR AWARENESS in a certain direction, you are in fact voting with your vibes. When you place your awareness on Love, you are Practicing the Presence.

One of the main skills of Practicing the Presence is the Awareness of Love. When Love is present, how do you feel? Calm, joyful, appreciated, relaxed, youthful, happy, peaceful, at ease, energized, relieved, poised ~ those are a few descriptors of what the Presence of Love feels like.

So it is good practice to notice throughout the day when you are feeling these things.

- **What are the thoughts accompanying these feelings?**
- **Is there any thought there at all?**
- **Can you remark upon a certain stillness that arises which feels perhaps transcendent in nature, when you are feeling Love's Presence?**

Your physical nature directly interfaces with these feelings. Your processor is equipped with certain functionalities which can inhibit or expand your awareness of Love's Presence. Your scientists remark on the various parts of the brain which elicit different responses based on various stimuli. You've likely heard of the fight or flight mechanism which increases blood flow and pumps in adrenalin, to prepare the vessel to be able to engage in a fight or run away when danger is sensed.

Due to the extreme nature of the generally unloving collective consciousness, many people experience living in the fight or flight stage for much too long, and, sometimes, never get a break from it. This wreaks havoc on the nervous system, and can cascade into numerous physical, mental, emotional, and spiritual ills over time.

The higher brain, called the cerebellum and cerebrum, opens us up to experience a state of peace and tranquility. This may also be called a state of Oneness or Unity, in which the perception of duality collapses, and the state of calm centeredness takes precedence. This is also the source of higher genius and intelligence.

From this state of calm centeredness, our perception changes, and it becomes easier to access our tools of Unconditional Love, Non-Judgment, Non-Attachment, and Non-Resistance. From this state of mind, it becomes natural to experience these things.

From the flight or fight state of mind, these experiences are difficult to reach. Even practiced persons under duress may succumb to non-loving thoughts and responses when they feel threatened. Sometimes there is an active threat, and other times, there is only the perception of a threat because of the conditioning of the mind from past experiences. Someone who has experienced abuse consistently might be in a continual mode of surveillance, wishing to avoid any surprise attack.

From what we've learned about the nature of reality, it becomes apparent that this person is going to experience more of the same—why? Because their thoughts through conditioning, are contemplating abuse and therefore, more is on its way.

It's like praying for what you don't want.

This is understandably a situation that elicits compassion, because you can see that the abused person is acting automatically from a conditioned response, and is most likely not aware of this fact. Much less are they aware of how their own processor is now causing new, unwanted experiences.

Perhaps their life stream guided them away from the original danger, but with every new relationship, somehow this energy surfaces, causing more grief and even despair over not knowing their way out of this trap.

This is indeed the birthing ground of compassion, as our hearts open wide to finally comprehend the nature of this suffering and where it came from. Love Itself reaches out to respond to this call of suffering and grief, and begins to dismantle its grip.

Awareness is the Master Key Code here which can begin to unlock the chambers of the heart and mind that have been sequestered by chemical overload from a tapped out nervous system, causing ever new cycling of experience along the same old story lines.

As awareness unlocks the truth behind our perception, we can question our own responses and notice whether they are coming from Truth or conditioning. This unlocking process takes time and awareness, and gets easier as we take the next step, and the next step, and the next.

Even advanced beings here in this earth plane are not immune to this graduation process. The conditioning has been building for eons in the collective consciousness, in particular in family lineages, and in the unique journeys of souls.

It is no wonder that there is such a plethora of self-help material coming through at this time to help humanity lift itself out of the murky waters of the past.

How can we train ourselves to become aware of Love's Presence, when emotional trigger responses arise?

STEP 1:

Become aware you are having a reaction. A conditioned response has arisen. Take note of it. Here are your tools:

- Refrain from judging yourself for having a reaction. Or if you can't, become non-resistant to the fact that you are in judgment of your reactions.

- Let go of attachment to outcome. In other words, don't worry whether you are going to be able to stop the reaction or not. Let it be. Feel the feelings.

- Practice loving yourself now. "Even though I am experiencing this trigger response, I am willing to love myself unconditionally."

The simple willingness itself opens the doors to love's bounteous nature of healing and restoration. Once you begin leveraging your awareness in this way, you will notice subtle shifts in your consciousness. You'll begin to notice that the Loving Awareness is indeed ever present, and with you every step of the way.

It always has been, you and others were just not always able to access it because of the state of the nervous system and running mind. This is why many spiritual systems rely on meditation as a core aspect of the training. Slowing down the nervous system and simply witnessing our own mind gets us into that state of Presence relatively quickly. Initiating your day with some form of practice is help to align and attune thought forms into higher vibrations, making it easier to notice when we are out of alignment or at risk to becoming triggered during the day. The truth is, being triggered ends up being a good thing, because it gives us the opportunity to become aware of how our conditioning works. Through this awareness, we begin to be able to make a choice, instead of running headlong into reactivity once again. Every time we make a new choice, we rewire our nervous system to a new pathway, which flows thought in more positive directions more easily, thereby energizing new outcomes in our lives which are more of a match to the loving harmony we desire and crave at very deep levels. We crave this harmony, because it is our own true nature. When we are out of touch with our true nature, we don't feel good. We are "out of sorts" or "beside ourselves."

This space of love called Awareness allows us to realign fully with the Truth of us. Over time, we become better and better at changing our responses, while simultaneously beginning to push the compounded momentum of our subconscious minds into new directions, bearing new results. This is how awareness feeds itself. The more you have, the more you have.

Now we can truly comprehend the meaning of the saying,

To those who have more, more shall be added.
To those who have not, even that
which they have shall be taken away.

~ Jesus

FINDING LOVE WITHIN YOURSELF

THE KINGDOM OF HEAVEN IS Your Awakened Consciousness. There are also myriad places in the heavens where the people are more aligned with Love's presence. These beings have simply awakened to a more advanced experience of knowing themselves as One with Source.

But what these beings in the "Many Mansions of the Father-Mother's House" have done, is to find the Presence of Love within themselves. Now, it is our turn, here on Earth. What we call Ascension or Graduation is at hand. But where are we ascending to, and what are we graduating from?

We are ascending to our higher consciousness, based on Love in the Heart Chakra, and we are graduating from the third dimensional classroom of life into the fourth dimensional classroom.* The third dimension correlates with the third chakra, the Solar Plexus. The lessons of the third chakra are self-differentiation, individuation, and personal power to choose one's own life direction. The shadow aspects of 3D are, correspondingly, egotism, greed, competition, and power over others. This is the place of control dramas on the one hand, and self-deprecation on the other. In its lightest and highest aspect, the 3D classroom gives us a healthy sense of boundaries, a sense of direction, and a purposefulness—a life's mission, if you will. It gives us a sense that we are powerful to make changes in the world, carving out our own niche and specialties in service to the whole.

In the Classroom of Ages, the light and dark aspects of the Lesson at hand are always present, displayed on the screen of the world, appearing as our experiences. The experiences are like the display monitor of our minds. We can see the state of our individual and collective consciousness by witnessing the state of our lives and our world.

Remember that much of the material informing this display screen exists in the subconscious mind instead of in our fully awakened conscious mind. Recall now that this material has come from compounded momentum in many directions:

- Our early conditioning
- The ongoing inputs of our culture
- Our ancestral lineage
- Our past lives and the levels of Soul Experience

Much of this conditioning is "as if invisible" because the mechanism of the conditioning itself makes it appear that these manifest things are normal and natural, so we get used to them and don't question them. This basically relegates them to what we call the unconscious or the subconscious. It is through our practice of Awareness that we begin to uncover these automated beliefs and thought forms to make a new decision, now consciously.

We must dig underneath them to discover the ever present nature of reality—the background energy of the Cosmos. In order to be able to do this, we have to have enough energy to choose away from distractions and move into contemplation of this underlying reality.

There are numerous practices and processes which can help one get aligned and attuned to Reality. It is a matter of tapping into the Heart, the very bosom of Love's residence. As we tap into the heart in one way or another, we gain access to the effulgent, effervescent, overflowing energy stream of pure divine love.

Note: There are many differing perspectives on the dimensions, which one we are shifting into and what that means. It is not the purpose of this book to argue a perspective on this, but to simply leverage the analogy for the purpose of growth.

EXERCISE 12: DISSOLVING OLD THOUGHT FORMS

The mind is overrated.
~ Dr. Kam Yuen

- Allow the mind to rest in the heart. Love the mind with all its busy-ness.
- Know that all is well as the mind is allowed to let go. The mind will be able to return to its processing. Now, we are going to tune into the heart of Pure Divine Love, which transcends the mind and its machinations.
- Find yourself penetrating the heart, more and more deeply. Imagine you are entering the deepest chambers of the Spiritual Energetic Heart Chakra.
- As you penetrate the deepest layer, you will feel, see or sense a spark of Light. This spark of Light is your original spirit spark which emanates from Source long, long ago—in terms of time.
- Allow this spark of Light to grow and expand, above, below, and all around about your aura now, filling your entire body, mind, emotions and spirit with this Light.
- Imagine that this ever filling love keeps pouring in to every crevice of your being. The golden-white sparkly light of your spirit is getting thicker, denser and more palpable as a radiant sun of pure divine love.
- Many things will start to happen as you rest in this love and this light. Your psychic intelligence will begin to kick in more strongly, making you aware of constructs or energetics in your mind-body- spirit complex.

- These now can be shifted through your awareness.
- If you see, sense or feel something "in there" that is not supposed to be there, you can basically love it into oblivion.
- How do you tell if it's "supposed to be there" or not? Basically, anything that stands out or has any shape or density, especially gray or black, is representing a construct not of your original pure golden light Source nature. You might sense, feel, see, or hear this energy. Some may even smell it. We are simply allowing the Power and Presence of Love to melt away anything that is "not us."

Remember, these constructs of the mind are causative to their own particular brand of chaos in our lives. They become like little magnets to experience, coded with the frequencies of the thoughts that created them.

We can begin to dismantle these thought constructs consciously now through our awareness, and the activation of the Presence of Love. We can simply allow our awareness to melt these constructs into oblivion, returning them to the nothingness from which they came. Then, it is easier for the being to make new decisions, because the constructs themselves are the representations of the compounded momentum of conditioning.

One by one and bit by bit, these constructs are dismantled and we become liberated to choose anew in every moment, now from a place of loving consciousness. The Awareness witnessing the constructs begins to dismantle them of its own accord. Remember that Pure Awareness is in fact the Power and Presence of Love, which:

- Does not judge
- Does not resist
- Is not attached
- Is unconditionally loving

This awareness enfolds these constructs within the fourfold embrace, and by nature, things begin to shift. Anything that is not of love simply fades away through the focus on Love's Presence.

Loving All That Is As It Is is one of the Master Key Codes to Healing and Recalibration

As a Source Streaming Human Angel, in your original nature, you are always streaming Source Energy. This means the effulgent, effervescent flow of divine love wisdom is on tap for you. Imagine floating in space as a human angel, and feeling the pulsations of this continual love-wisdom vibration moving through you. This is endless primordial energy, and in your angelic human form, you are designed to stream Source all the time. The outer form of the angelic human is like your wetsuit in the Ocean of Love, allowing you to traverse myriad realms with ease.

Behind you is all the data of all your lineages and experiences, and before you are the many possibilities from which you are continually able to choose. Love flows freely in you, as you, to you, and through you, hearkening to the next adventure, and always again, the next adventure.

Since there are no obstructions in your awareness, you are constantly aware of yourself as One with Source. This means a continual feeling of exhilaration, readiness, poise and grace, as you sense the ever present Love of All That Is.

Tapping into this Original aspect of self, your true divine nature, you as an Earth human can become more and more At One with this Grace of this Eternal Love.

Even while we are on the path of recalibrating to our full awareness of this Love, we can see and feel changes occurring in our perception and thus know there will be new results in our lives.

EXERCISE 13: IMAGINE YOURSELF AS A SOURCE STREAMING HUMAN ANGEL

Imagine yourself as a Source Streaming Human Angel. Imagine you can see and feel the entire array of past experiences, wisdom and knowledge displayed behind you. In your multidimensional awareness, whatever strand of information you focus on comes to life.

- **What stands out as important for you to know about your past?**

Whatever you are shown, will have some significance to your path of healing right now. **Write your responses in your journal.**

Now imagine that an entire array of possibilities is spread out before you. Imagine that you can see or feel these possibilities as lines of light in varying shades of dark to light. As you scan them, one stands out brighter than the rest. Place your attention on that one, and intend to receive information about this life possibility before you. What does it tell you? **Write your responses in your journal.**

Know that this is a probable or possible timeline for you. As you stay aligned with the Power of Love's Presence in you, you are more and more likely to ride the wave of this lightest timeline.

Feel the exhilaration of streaming Source through your very being. Allow that Light which is Love to rejuvenate, cleanse and heal you. Allow your mind to imagine the possibilities of this timeline of Love's choosing.

- What are its highlights?
- What happens as the vision expands in you?

Write your responses in your journal.

Note: It will take concentration to keep your focus on the new, desired timeline. Treat this focus like the most precious thing that belongs to you.

EXERCISE 14: FINDING LOVE WITHIN YOU

Invoking Love's Presence

Read the following statement aloud or silently, and feel free to change the wording to your preference:

- Divine Creator, Source, Power and Presence of Love, I am so grateful to Know we are One.
- Thank you for helping me to comprehend our Oneness, more and more each day.
- Help me to bask in the Knowing that All Is Well, as I change and adapt my thoughts to meet Your Divine Vibrations, which are my true and original vibrations.

Source's Perspective of You

The vibrational emanations of Source as Love are never-ending. These Source emanations are the very nature of empowerment and enlivenment for all that is. As the Power behind the Manifestations, this Source has also created us, and we therefore have endless access to this stream of love. We can learn how to direct it to bless our lives and heal our world.

Not only is this an opportunity for us, it is part of our design, our function, to be at the helm of our world and create beauty here.

> **There are no passengers on spaceship Earth. We are all crew.**
> —*Marshall McLuhan*

From the Source Perspective of the Original Prime Creator, you are a powerful, purposeful, vibrant, pulsating Light. This Light as Love that you are has extended itself unto creation such that the Primordial Consciousness can experience Itself from numerous perspectives.

Thus this Original Source Consciousness perceives You as Itself. As the foundation of You, this Source knows everything about you—where you came from, where you are going, who you were in your previous lives, which hurts still bother you, where your blockages are, how they got there, and how to heal them in the most loving ways.

This Source also knows your True Divine Mission and Purpose—the calling for which you were indeed created, in essence, as an Extension of Source.

This Source as parent, masquerading as you, thus loves you beyond any comprehension of Love that human beings typically imagine from ordinary consciousness. Allowing the fullness of this Love to flower within you, creates a blossoming forth into a richer expression of your true divine magnificence. This Source is always on tap, always available—ever present. You can reach out to it, reach into it, bask in it, allow it to fill you — and play in the energy of it any time you choose.

Since Source Energy as Love is truly All There Is, we can find a safe haven of trust within its bosom.

Furthermore, since this is on tap, why not tap into it and live your Life as Source? If this *is* the Primordial Energy of Creation, why would we *not* tap into this Effulgent Stream, continually nourishing and replenishing ourselves? Why would we initiate anything without tapping into it? If this is your true nature, then you do not have to go through any intermediary to attain connection with Source. In fact, you cannot help but be it, as you are it. It is simply a matter of refining and redirecting our consciousness to continually tap into and return to this awareness of Love's Presence for creating what we desire and solving any problem.

This exercise is more simple than meets the eye, yet could feel difficult from your ordinary perception. This is why it is paramount to have in your arsenal a variety of shift tools that help you make the switch to the vibration and consciousness of Love. This consciousness can then direct you because you will be in vibrational proximity to it, and therefore able to receive the message.

When you feel disconnected, it's like a cell phone that is away from all cell phone towers. There is no reception because the frequency bandwidth is not in range.

Meditation, reflection, dance, pausing, making art, making love, and focusing on love — these are all ways to realign and re-attune to love's vibratory signature so you can receive messages and wisdom directly. It may feel difficult to pull away from regular activities that have become a pattern. You may have to make an effort to do so. Making a decision that you are willing to give yourself this play and freedom, opens up the energy and makes it easier to do something different.

When we seek the advice of counselors, mystics, psychics and healers, we are simply tethering our connection to someone who temporarily has a stronger, more direct connection that is decluttered. They do not have your subconscious debris in their filter, though they may be able to detect it on your behalf.

Just remember that a true teacher, guru, or healer will always redirect you back to your own Inner Source Connection, to empower you — not to keep you coming back and making you a slave to third party information. It is always wonderful and divine to have those reflections in life, through people who can share and bask in Divine Love Wisdom, helping you interpret incoming energies properly. With so much distraction in the culture and consciousness, this is a precious gift.

Just be aware of any level of attachment to a particular channel or source of information, and continually strive to make the deep authentic connection with your own divine nature — Source—The Love Within You, primary.

Sometimes nature and the animal kingdom will rally to help you.

The signs and symbols from your Inner Spirit are all around you. When animals seem to do something unusual, it is oftentimes a symbolic attempt to reach your conscious mind with information.

If you don't know what it means, don't worry. Just ask for Life Itself to reveal the message to you. Now that you have symbols such as how many animals were there, what color they were, which direction were they coming from and heading to, Life will fill in the blanks and reveal the message in divine order.

For a complimentary guided meditation related to this chapter, called **Find Your True Love Within,** *please visit Chireya.com/love-book.*

PRINCIPLES TO LIVE BY

Forgiveness is King and Queen, and Reigns Supreme

CAN WE NOW COMPREHEND forgiveness better, since we understood the dynamics of how experience transpires? When we forgive, is this to say that what the other does is right or good? Or is forgiveness shifting our perspective, so we can see the nature of things as they are, thereby becoming non-resistant, unconditionally loving, non-judgmental, and unattached?

Unconditional Love as Forgiveness births Non-Judgment, Non-Attachment, And Non-Resistance

Unconditional Love is the parent of Forgiveness. Together, they give rise to Non-Judgment, Non-Resistance, and Non- Attachment. These are not mere transcendental notions devoid of feeling. To the contrary, these are activations of the Love Principle in the Most High.

The Love Principle

Love Source Entirely. This is the Essence of Falling in Love with the Beloved Within. As you Love Source, you Love Yourself—ALL of Yourself.

Love Your Neighbor as Yourself. Your neighbor *is* Your Self in a different costume. What goes out of you, comes back to you. This is the Law of Life. When you LOVE your neighbor as yourself, this means you have the conscious awareness of your Intrinsic Oneness. Your Intrinsic Oneness hearkens to the Reality behind appearances of the illusion that you and your neighbor are separate. When you embrace the Love Principle, you will not be able to harm anyone.

The Principle of Individuation

As an expression—a Source Seed—of God Consciousness, you embody a unique perspective enjoyed by All That Is. Your unique expression is a delight—it is delightful to the Love Behind All Things that you exist.

> **Personally, it is my conviction that all sentient beings are immortal spiritual beings. This includes human beings. For the sake of accuracy and simplicity I will use a made-up word: 'IS-BE'. Because the primary nature of an immortal being is that they live in a timeless state of 'is', and the only reason for their existence is that they decide to 'be'. No matter how lowly their**

station in a society, every IS-BE deserves the respect and treatment that I myself would like to receive from others. Each person on Earth continues to be an IS-BE whether they are aware of the fact or not.
~ Alien Interview

The Principle of Freedom

You are free to choose, free to be, free to rest, free to love, free to express. You were created this way, so this elemental freedom is a part of your inheritance and birthright. The Free Will Anchor in this particular reality is backed up by the Law of Life—that which goes around comes around.

The Law of Life

Anchored and tethered by the Law, the Source expanded and individuated for the purpose of exploration. Knowing that the individuated aspect would always have the reflection of "what they were putting out," Prime Creator felt ready to embark on this mysterious journey called Creation. You as an Aspect of this Source are not immune to the functions of the Law. In fact, it is your tether and your rope to conscious living. As you embrace the Law as Lord, Ruler of All — i.e., the "Rules of the Game," this gives you the stability with which to navigate in your magnificent existence. In order to fully embrace the divine gift that this is, there are some things you would naturally give up:

1. Your perception that you are a victim of life.
2. Your judgments of others and yourself.
3. Your thought that you are separate from Love, or have been abandoned. (This engenders "trust".)

Giving up these three things may feel unsettling at first. Allow this unsettling feeling to turn into a feeling of expectancy. Once you have claimed and decided you are going to live in this way, Love Itself will support and guide you through the steps necessary for full alignment with this gift.

EXERCISE 15: SUMMING IT UP

Write your responses in your journal.

Does it feel difficult to take full responsibility for your existence? Is it hard to let go of the role of victim in any area of life?

What is harder — letting go of judgment of yourself, or of others?

Are you ready to embrace the Knowing that you have never been abandoned by Life, and you never will be? Is there any resistance present to this level of trust? If so, write it out:

EXERCISE 16: DECLARE WILLINGNESS

**Are you willing to give up:
FEAR, VICTIMHOOD, JUDGMENTS,
BELIEFS IN UNWORTHINESS
to the Creator within you?**

If YES, take a moment NOW to stand before the Truth of Yourself.

Declare:

Divine Presence of Love!

I now cast the burden of these old ways, unto your Light, Love, & Truth. As the Real Me, You know what I need now, Creator. Though it may feel uncomfortable, I am willing to scrape the bottom of the barrel of any beliefs I hold that are not aligned with Love. Creator, hold my hand and embrace me with all your love as I dismantle the outworn notions of the old consciousness, and become a forerunner to the awakened consciousness of humanity now. I do this not as a sacrifice, because there is nothing to lose except delusion, and nothing to gain but the truth of me.

Help me and stand by me, even when memories of my past human weakness, fears, foibles, challenges, patterns, and beliefs surface.

I am willing to extend trust to You, Source, in tender ways, to make my way back gently to full realization of myself as One with You.

Thank you God-Source-Love,
Thank you God-Source-Love,
Thank you God-Source-Love,
So be it, and so it is!

Note: As always, substitute your preferred word for God-Source-Love as desired.

BE IN LOVE WITH THE BELOVED WITHIN

REST IN THE KNOWING that All Is Well. Your Divine Source Consciousness is ever present and cannot be taken from you. Neither can it be changed, broken, or deranged.

It is the Seat of All Existence, and that which backs it up. It is the Permanent Reality underneath this so called reality of continual change. An array of experiences, likes, loves, people, places and things play out before your eyes. Love them. They all came from You (the Big You), and they will all return there as well. There is nothing to do but Love. There is nowhere to be but Here.

Practicing these Truths in a daily existence filled with many agenda items and unending creative thought streams, can seem challenging.

This is why they call it the straight and narrow path.

It is straight because it leads to only one place — Love's truth of you. It is narrow as a gift of love, to keep you navigating correctly. The Truth is, you have all the time in the world to get there. Everyone will return Home to Love, eventually.

When you are ready, you will take up the Mantle of this Work, of your own accord. Until then, know that All Is Well, that Love, Light, and Truth are always there to guide you—Ever present, All Knowing, and All Powerful.

You are a beautiful and unique creator of Love. This Love will never abandon you. It is only you who can abandon yourself— albeit temporarily.

> **When you are ready, you will know.**
> **When you are ready, you will grow.**
> **When you are ready, you will heal.**
> **The time is now, to know what's real.**

LOVE IS. YOU ARE. AND ALL IS WELL.

AFTERWORD
ARE YOU THE MINI ME OF SOURCE?

Fun Facts of Creation and Background Info for Advanced Students as To The Origin of the Fountainhead of Creation

THE PRESENCE ITSELF DOES the healing. The Presence Itself does the awakening. The Presence Itself does the recalibration. The Presence Itself sets all into divine order. This is how it works. We are Extensions of this Source Creator in form, here to have a phenomenal experience of Life Itself while learning the Codes of the Divine Creator in an experiential classroom bar none.

Never had there been such a grand experiment attempted, never had the Prime Creator launched Itself into such an amazing, incredible, awesome, and phenomenal Creation for the purpose of self-expression, self- awareness, self-love, and self-realization.

At the core, you are the Source. At the expression level, you are an emanation of the Source, a being of light, a spark of light, that was birthed from the lovemaking of the Divine Father and Divine Mother in the Template / Temple of Creation Itself.

The divine secret sanctuary or Template / Temple of the Divine Mother and Divine Father was created upon the desire of the Source Creator to have an experience in a phenomenological creation.

The phenomenological creation is an expression of electrical vibratory love pulsations, coming from within the hearth-heart of the Divine Mother and Divine Father in full communion with One Another and the Primordial Pre-existent Unity we call Source.

This Pre-existent Unity is everywhere expressed, even though it is self-cloaked in circumstances for the purpose of learning, growth and expansion. We can now see that this Primordial Source Itself desired to have this experience, and therefore emanated itself into time and space as the polar unity of Divine Mother and Divine Father.

This is represented in the yin-yang symbol.

As many great physicists are realizing in our day, the Divine Union of the polar opposites of Divine Mother and Divine Father, Yin and Yang, dark and light, positive and negative—generates a polar differential expression, manifesting as a generative engine, which births all of creation into form.

This polarity-in-unity creates a cycling effect, which generates energy from the flipping and spiraling that manifests from the actual polar occurrence itself. The spin that occurs from this original Source Energy and Essence of Divine Mother — Divine Father lovemaking, created the space in which all of creation exists.

This is the Temple of which we speak. So the temple or template emanates from this generative, gyrating, spiral energy flow. This is the Grid of Creation, the Pattern or Platform upon which Existence can occur.

Here you also find Energy Itself being birthed into time and space, for the purpose of animating beings and things. This magneto- electric polar force generates the energy necessary to sustain a creation.

From their love making, another occurrence that takes place is that of sparks of light flying off into space as emanations of the One into many smaller versions.

This is us. We are truly the Mini Me of Source! Love yourself! ;)

And so it is.

STAND NAKED TO THE TRUTH

Disrobing from the detritus caused
by effects of past impulses,
we stand naked to the
Truth of us.

Standing naked to the Truth of us,
we see, know and feel ourselves as
One with Source.

Seeing, knowing and feeling
ourselves as
One with Source,
we weep with gratitude at the
magnificence of creation.

Weeping with gratitude at the
magnificence of creation,
we love ourselves back into holiness.

Loving ourselves back into holiness,
we cannot help but love all beings
back into

Wholeness and Oneness.

Loving all beings back into
Wholeness and Oneness,
we redeem our causative
emanations
with wholehearted compassion.

Redeeming our causative
emanations
with wholehearted compassion,
we free all beings from suffering.

Freeing all beings from suffering,
we reunite with the Beloved
in every encounter.

Reuniting with the Beloved
in every encounter,
we collapse duality and don't mind
one bit,
that we stand Naked, to the
Truth of us.

ABOUT THE AUTHOR

FOUNDER OF THE Life Architecture Academy, Chireya Fox is an Intuitive Guide, Life Design Specialist, and orator and scribe for the Lineages of Light. She brings forth wisdom teachings for the purpose of helping people awaken to the Truth of us. We are One with Source. Now, let's KNOW this. Her desire is that all beings may come to know and fall in love with the love within. She asks us to imagine what the world will be like, when everyone does this. For complimentary Guided Meditation Audios and to discover more about Chireya and her programs, visit **Chireya.com/Love-Book.**

TO RECEIVE THE EXERCISES IN THIS BOOK AS A FREE PRINTABLE .PDF FILE, PLEASE VISIT
CHIREYA.COM/LOVE-EXERCISES

www.ingramcontent.com/pod-product-compliance
Lightning Source LLC
LaVergne TN
LVHW011209080426
835508LV00007B/694